hen

poule

rooster

coq

chick

poussin

duckling

caneton

turkey

dinde

donkey

âne

swan

cygne

frog

grenouille

racoon

raton laveur

bear

ours

squirrel

écureuil

fly

mouche

ladybug

coccinelle

worm

ver

snail

escargot

slug

limace

bee

abeille

spider

araignée

beetle

scarabée

dragonfly

libellule

lion

lion

zebra

zèbre

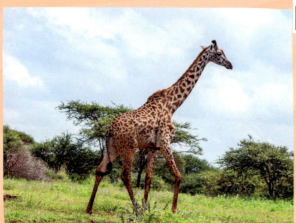

giraffe

girafe

rhinoceros

rhinocéros

snake

serpent

mosquito

🇫🇷 **moustique**
🇨🇦 **maringouin**

sea turtle

tortue de mer

hippopotamus

hippopotame

alligator

alligator

crocodile

crocodile

shark

requin

walrus

morse

penguin

pingouin

polar bear

ours polaire

seal

phoque

starfish

étoile de mer

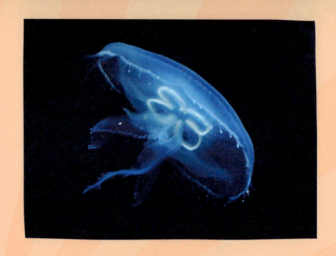

jellyfish

méduse

seashells

coquillages

feather

plume

11
eleven

onze

12
twelve

douze

13
thirteen

treize

14
fourteen

quatorze

15

fifteen

quinze

16

sixteen

seize

17

seventeen

dix-sept

18

eighteen

dix-huit

19

nineteen

dix-neuf

20

twenty

vingt

heart

cœur

oval

ovale

arrow

flèche

crescent

croissant

curve

courbe

spiral

spirale

cross

croix

zigzag

zigzag

rainbow

arc en ciel

dark colors

couleurs foncées

light colors

couleurs claires

dots

points

line

ligne

short

petit

tall

grand

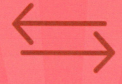

a little

a lot

un peu

beaucoup

full

empty

rempli

vide

curly hair

cheveux bouclés

straight hair

🇫🇷 cheveux raides
🇨🇦 cheveux droits

accept

accepter

refuse

refuser

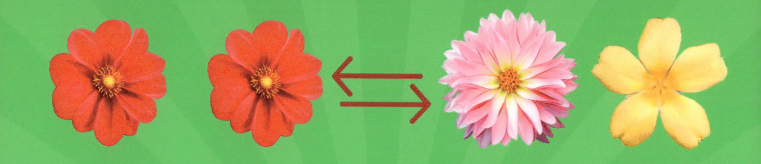

identical

identique

different

différent

dry

sec

wet

mouillé

toys

jouets

blocks

cubes

ball

ballon

robots

robots

tongue

langue

nose

nez

hair

cheveux

moustache

moustache

fingers

doigts

arm

bras

knee

genou

elbow

coude

smile

sourire

kiss

bisou

cry

pleurer

pain

douleur

body

corps

back

dos

pacifier

🇫🇷 tétine

🇨🇦 suce

high chair

chaise haute

soap

savon

toothbrush

brosse à dents

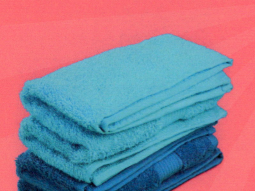

towel

serviette

potty

🇫🇷 **pot**
🇨🇦 **petit pot**

ring

bague

bracelet

bracelet

necklace

collier

earring

boucle d'oreille

chocolate

chocolat

popcorn

pop-corn

jam

confiture

toast

tartine

honey

miel

butter

beurre

bread

pain

ice cream

🇫🇷 glace
🇨🇦 crème glacée

semolina

semoule

rice

riz

pasta

pâtes

soup

soupe

milk

lait

water

eau

juice

jus

kiwi

kiwi

raspberry

framboise

grapefruit

pamplemousse

melon

🇫🇷 melon
🍁 melon miel

plum

prune

apricot

abricot

pomegranate

grenade

fig

figue

blueberry

🇫🇷 **myrtille**
🇨🇦 **bleuet**

cranberry

canneberge

persimmon

kaki

lychee

litchi

fruits

fruits

vegetables

légumes

avocado

avocat

green bean

haricot vert

broccoli

brocoli

eggplant

aubergine

peas

petits pois

bell pepper

poivron

beet

betterave

lettuce

🇫🇷 salade
🇨🇦 laitue

endive

endive

artichoke

artichaut

leek

poireau

onion

oignon

garlic

ail

ginger

gingembre

walnuts

noix

almond

amande

pistachio

pistache

cashew

noix de cajou

Made in United States
Cleveland, OH
22 December 2024